THE
GIFT

The Twenty Seconds
That Changed My Life.

David Williams

MINDSTIR MEDIA

The Gift

Copyright © 2022 by David Williams. All rights reserved.

No part of this book may be used or reproduced in any manner whatsoever without written permission, except in the case of brief quotations embodied in critical articles and reviews. For more information, e-mail all inquiries to info@mindstirmedia.com.

Published by Mindstir Media, LLC
45 Lafayette Rd | Suite 181| North Hampton, NH 03862 | USA
1.800.767.0531 | www.mindstirmedia.com

Printed in the United States of America
ISBN-13: XXX-X-XXXXXXX-X-X

PREFACE

When I decided to jot down my memoirs, it was intended to help me release a hold I had on my past. It took me a long time to get the courage to tell my story. There are definitely ups and downs. This book is a collage of unfiltered mishaps and memories and my struggle for survival.

I needed an outlet to rid myself of the intense anxiety I had inside of me. What it actually did was bring the memories alive. It activated my brain into full power mode and spit out everything that I have tried to suppress over the years. It scared me at first but enlightened me as well. There were moments and events I had totally forgotten about, and for good reason. The child abuse, which was verbal and physical and emotional, the relentless, intense bullying throughout my school years that broke my spirit and has scarred me for life, the dysfunctional family life, the dysfunctional life that I made even worse as I got older because I relied on other people to help me when I could have done it myself. I witnessed an incredible supernatural event when I was nearly six years old, and that event has changed my life dramatically. I have a slight addiction to playing the lottery hoping to land a windfall so I may retire in real style. It's only recently I've realized that I've already won the lottery, just not with money. I won it when I was six years old on that splendid night. Since that incredible evening I have not really wanted anything, been watched over constantly, mysteriously dodged bullets from the AIDS pandemic as well as Covid19 (amid other close calls), and I have finally found peace and love. At sixty-five years old,

I live with my husband that I have known for over forty years. I've finally found peace and I am grateful to Jesus for that mystical gift on that moonlit evening that he chose for me to receive and everything he has given me through the years. And I mean…Many thanks!

INTRODUCTION

My name is David Williams. This book is a collage of my memories from my childhood until today. Writing this book has been incredibly healing but so hard. I am not a seasoned writer by any means and don't profess to be one. I wrote what came to mind but I did have to dig deep for a lot of the works. Some of the memories are hurtful and some are wonderful. I've realized and learned an important lesson that life is very short and should be lived to the fullest. The past cannot always be forgotten and can be very painful, especially when digging up old memories, but this was needed to be done to complete this overdue project. So many people have played a role in my small life. When I say small, I mean I have not achieved what many great people have done that I have known…but my life, even as small as it is, is important. It's taken me years to realize that and to realize I really do matter.

CHAPTER ONE

EARLY YEARS

In the beginning, God created the Heavens and Earth. I was born in late January, 1956. It was a bitter cold winter morning. My mother's name was Dorothy, and she was nearly seven months pregnant and forty-six years old. She was bringing in laundry that was hung out to dry the day before when she slipped and fell on the ice coming up the back porch stairs. She was rushed to Saugus General Hospital in Saugus, MA. I was born by caesarian section about two hours later. Being over two months premature and weighing only a little over three pounds, I remained in the hospital for about three weeks before going home to our Saugus, Massachusetts Central Street apartment. My sister Carol, who was nineteen years old at the time, lived with my mother and myself then and off and on for many years later. When I was about three months old, I was baptized at St. John's Episcopal Church in Saugus. Baptism is common but what is not common is to vividly remember the service itself as a baby. I can. I remember being carried in by Harry, my sister Jean's first husband. Later in life I brought this up to my mother and sisters Jean and Carol. They were stunned that I knew that and other things throughout the service that day that I could not have ever known…It is very odd.

We moved from that small apartment on Central Street to a larger apartment on Vine Street in Saugus when I was five years old. I also entered kindergarten that year. It was 1961. I remember it clearly. The warm milk, stale animal-shaped cookies and grouchy older women teachers with little patience. It was in a small rustic Cape Cod-style house not far from our Vine Street apartment. My mother had an old French Canadian dear friend named Frenchie who would pick me up because my mother and Carol worked. He was a rough individual. Very nice to me and my mother though. An auto mechanic by heart and a kind soul in general.

Both my mother and Carol had full time jobs. My mother was a secretary for United Farmers in nearby Lynn, and Carol a nurse at Saugus General Hospital where I was born. My father, whose name was Claude, was not in the picture. He was a gambling alcoholic with a quick temper. My mother had married about a year before I was born. It was her second marriage and it was clearly a mistake on her part. He tried to reconcile numerous times but my mother would not stand for it. He was never a part of our lives. I was taken care of throughout the day by one of my mother's dearest friends. Her name was Margie but all the kids called her Nana. She was a widow in her sixties and was a lovely, kind woman who had a beautiful, giant old home in Saugus. She was a great cook and loved being a homemaker because she had many children of her own along with foster kids and children like me that she babysat. I can remember waking up from naps to the Art Linkletter show on many chilly fall and winter days. What a great flashback. My mother would pick me up early in the evening and take me home to our Vine Street apartment with my supper that Nana would have made for me, packed up so nicely.

My stay at Nana's wasn't always sweet though. Nana took in foster kids. Sometimes three or four at a time. One afternoon Nana left one of the boys to watch me while she went to do some errands for a bit. He was about sixteen years old or so and I was about five years old. I remember vividly him making me perform oral sex on him. It was really quick. It was also in the dining room where there were windows on the side where people entered so he could see anybody coming. I remember him doing it twice. I never told anyone. I thought my mother would get angry with me and I would have to stop going to Nana's and I loved going there. I just kept it my secret inside of me all these years and never told anyone. It feels good to let it out now.

– CHAPTER ONE –

PART TWO

THE GIFT

One evening back in the summer of 1961, when I was about six years old, I remember vividly a very strange happening. It was a clear, beautiful evening and my mother was working late. I believe my sister Carol was at a Tupperware or Fuller Brush or whatever kind of party at the downstairs neighbor's apartment. I heard an enormous clap of thunder. The kind of thunder that rocks the house. I didn't see any lightning, but I was drawn to the side window in the living room by the thunder. I saw an enormous supermoon surrounded by clouds, and as plain and clear as day I can remember seeing a large figure of a man walking in the clouds. He was bright and very luminous. I wasn't sure at first what or who it was. But I know one thing: it was not my imagination. To this day, I have a firm recollection of this event and I remember it clearly. I very clearly have that image planted in my mind. Not one day has gone by in over sixty years since it happened that I don't think of it. Not one day. The man was dressed in a white robe with a dark beard. And again, he was so bright white and it was eerie. He was not looking at me. He was walking very slowly and gradually disappeared into the clouds as they moved and I was sad when I lost sight of him. It lasted about twenty seconds. It wasn't until many years later that I realized how those twenty seconds were to dramatically change my life.

About a month after I witnessed this apparition or whatever it was, we moved to Lynn. My father started to come around the Vine St Saugus apartment to visit and my mother wanted no part of him. He was a drunken gambler who brought her nothing but grief. We quickly moved to Lynn, Massachusetts early one Saturday morning. My father never appeared again. The Lynn apartment was dingy and on an undesirable street. We only lived there for six months before moving to Georgetown, MA, where my other sister Jean who was twenty-three years old had just bought a new house with her new husband Hank who was nearly double her age. While in Lynn though, a strange thing happened one morning. My mother and I were preparing to go shopping. Our apartment was on the second floor and the stairs that led down to the front entrance were treacherous. Many old-fashioned wood stairs with no carpet. My mother was waiting for me down at the front door. I was rushing and lost my footing. I went headfirst down the stairs, hitting my head and neck on every single stair going down. My mother was hysterical. When I got to the bottom of the stairs, she knew I had probably broken my neck at the very least, if not died. I was fine. No injury whatsoever. She didn't believe me. I can remember her screaming, "Turn your neck!! Turn your neck!!" I did. Nothing was wrong. She said, "This is impossible!" I said again to her, "I am fine." I actually remember hitting each stair. It was as if I was in a bubble of some sort. No pain whatsoever and cushioned somehow. It was very weird. I know now that this was a total divine intervention. No way anything else would have saved me. I had no injury whatsoever from this very dangerous mishap.

Little did I realize that this incident when I should have clearly been very physically injured was only the first to be among others to come later in my life that I believe are directly associated with those twenty seconds on that night when I saw that strange man walking in the clouds. But I always ask myself…Why? Why me?

– CHAPTER TWO –

GEORGETOWN

We lived in Lynn for about six months. We moved to my sister Jean and her husband Hank's house in Georgetown, MA. The house was new and nice. I started first grade later that year as well. It was January 1962. Shortly after moving to my sister Jean and her husband Hank's house. Jean was twenty-three years old and Hank was forty-four. I knew it was bad. They fought constantly over money. They were living way beyond their means financially. Jean had a brand new Cadillac and they both spent tons of money on fabulous furniture and an expensive organ as well as a built-in swimming pool. They also had a three-stall stable built in the backyard, complete with a furnished tack room for saddles and three gorgeous horses. Way over the top for Jean's salary. Hank never finished the third grade and was in and out of jobs. Hank inherited about $50,000.00 when he married Jean and they blew right through it. My mother helped out here and there and paid rent to them as well. It wasn't enough. The fighting continued and escalated from just verbal to full-blown physical fighting. My sister woke up in the morning more than once with black eyes. I remember one particular night when I thought he was going to kill her. I was alone with them, my mother was working late, and Jean got a brutal beating from Hank. To this day I can still hear her screaming for help. I was nine years old at the time. They had been fighting most of the evening, lashing out back and forth. Finally, she picked up a heavy alabaster stone ashtray and threw it at him while he was shaving. He went nuts and I ran upstairs. Then the fists started to fly. I went back down to help her and he was trying to put her head sideways on the electric stove burner and wanted me to turn it on. I screamed, "NO. Let her go!" He did. This fight lasted about a half an hour. My mother came home and things settled down and we went to bed. These events were daily and getting more abusive as time went on. Constant bickering and fights and hatred filled the house. It was pure torment just living there. The swearing and the arguing was in the house and out in the backyard. It was everywhere. it was so embarrassing with the neighbors and the neighbors complained numerous times and called the police as well. My childhood was always traumatic. My teen years were terrible. My mother was always sick. My father bolted because my mother basically threw him out. So it was a lousy childhood. I really missed out. Finally, I am happy now. But I must say my faith in Jesus has saved me over the years. The apparition was a true miracle. I want to spread the word that Jesus totally exists. He really does. I saw it for myself.

My sister Jean had a horrible childhood. My mother left her when she was seven years old with a friend of hers while she ran off for Florida during the winter months. She was a waitress and made awesome cash catering to rich men in Palm Beach. This lasted from December until April. She left poor Jean with Margie (Nana) while she was gone, and Carol was staying with another one of my mother's friends. When I came into the picture, my mother was over the Florida stuff and treated me beautifully. Jean was always noticeably resentful. Jean did not always treat me nice and did cruel things to me. I remember once going to bed and was just about to fall asleep when Jean and Hank had come home with an adult male German Shepherd they had adopted from the local Army base. It was vicious. She knew I was frightened of dogs and especially this one and she opened my bedroom door and sent him in and closed the door. I was stricken with fear. I couldn't move in bed. The room was pitch black and I could smell the dog's breath and hear his growling. I knew I would surely be attacked. I could hear Jean laughing hysterically outside my room. The dog simply laid down on the floor and went to sleep.

We had an inground pool that was so much fun but Jean used to like to torment me when I went in. I was afraid of the water and drowning so I was always cautious. She used to take my legs and twirl me around so my head was underwater and gulping in tons of water while I had no way to get out. It was basically waterboarding. It made me not use the pool for the fear of torture.

My days at school were tough. I was obviously a little slow but very smart as well, but no one spoke of it. I realized later in life that I am slightly savant, having an incredible memory and being able to play any song on the piano after only listening to it once. I knew I was different in another way as well but did not know what gay meant. I was obviously feminine and could not hide it. The three-mile school bus ride was hell. Then I arrived in total hell. I was made fun of, kicked, spat on, strangled, slapped across the face, and brutally tormented from the moment I arrived till the moment I left. Then the abusive school bus ride back home and then the fighting began with Jean and Hank each and every night. I had no safe haven. It was pure torment day after day and night after night. On weekends I would help out with chores while my sister played records on the console stereo. Tunes like Brenda Lee's "I'm Sorry" were "always a Saturday hit" favorite. Horrible! But as an added twist, I listen to the same songs today that I despised then. My sister was into horses and animals. We had a stable with three horses, a couple goats, and about 200 chickens. Another two dogs and three cats. I helped out with the feeding and cleaning. This was the best part of living there. I loved the animals as long as the two-legged ones stayed clear. My sister Jean was always getting new animals. We had a mishap one night though. One of the dogs "Comet" was a full-grown German Shepard. He was in the corral with one of the horses one early evening and he attacked the horse. I thought it was odd because he was so gentle, but animals can be unpredictable, especially certain breeds. The horse had to be put down because of the injuries to its legs. My sister went ballistic and beat up Comet with the blunt end of a hammer. I witnessed it and the dog yelping so loud in pain. I never forgot that moment. Comet was never put down but never attacked anything again. If you even reached for a hammer for anything, you wouldn't see him for an hour. Speaking of hammers, Hank traded in his usual Chevy pickup truck after it needed too much work, so he went and bought a used Datsun pickup truck. I believe Datsun is now Nissan. The Datsun was much smaller but still was a hefty, little truck. It did everything the Chevy pickup did that Hank needed it for. Getting Hay and food supplies for Jean's horses and chickens and goats and sheep and everything else she had. But oh no Jean was not happy with the Datsun. Hank had actually bought it behind her back. To make matters worse, he wasn't thrilled with the plain white color it came with. So he had some leftover house paint but the color was hideous. It was pumpkin orange. I have no idea what he used it for before. Maybe the window shutters. But he painted his new Datsun with it. Hank, as you can see, was crazy. Jean sees the new painted Datsun and goes nuts! She grabbed a hammer from the garage and went on a smashing parade. The truck was all smashed in on the side and the room and the headlights. She was nuts too. Hank saw this and grabbed the hammer from her and smashed it in her new Cadillac. Just a typical Saturday afternoon!

Years went by; summers went by. One summer my mother saved up and bought a pony for me. I was scared to ride horses so she thought the pony would be a good idea to get me used to it. He was whitish silver color and was cute. I named him Silver. One early evening during the summer I rode him in the backyard. Jean and Hank's house was on nearly three acres so there was plenty of space to ride. I was going slow because I was nervous. Jean comes over and says "C'Mon" speed it up. I didn't want to. Silver was a little skittish and Jean took a branch and switched him on the ass. He took off. I lost my balance and fell off. I thought I either broke or dislocated my shoulder. I was screaming in pain. Jean simply walked away, never checking to see if I was okay. Totally did not care and I could see her laughing hysterically. My mother took back Silver to where she bought him the next day. Jean could be very cruel. My shoulder mysteriously healed shortly after. I was fine.

My mother made me go to Sunday school. It was horrible but wonderful. I met so many great people. My mother and I attended the First Baptist Church in Georgetown, MA. The Reverend was such a wonderful man. He was a very nice family man. Always had a great sermon. I was picked up by a very old-aged, yellow school bus the church had bought to pick up kids for Sunday school and mostly elderly people who did not drive. It was fun to talk and listen to their stories they told en route to church. There was an older couple that owned a mink farm that joined us on the bus. They always smelled like the minks. They were so nice though. Their home was in the woods a bit and looked so creepy. I can remember Christmas caroling with the church around the holidays. I was hesitant at first because I can't really sing. I went anyway. The elderly people in the nursing home loved it. Christmas time at Jean and Hank's was always turmoil. There were plenty of presents under the tree but no love in the air. My mother tried so hard to make it nice though. But there was always a Jean and Hank fight. Sometimes right at the holiday dinner table. You never knew when it was coming until it came. Hank would curl his lip, Jean would start cursing, and the dishes and food started flying. Horrible. I have nice memories of my mother and I driving very early on Saturday mornings to go get meat and veggies in Boston at Haymarket Square. My mother had her favorite guys for chicken and pork and her guys for veggies. We would go to the Pilgrim market in the basement, which was covered in sawdust on the floor. I can still remember that smell. She would take me to a diner at the end of the market that no longer exists. The new Bostonian Hotel now sits at that spot. I can also remember warm summer nights going to the Hammond Castle in Gloucester, MA for beautiful organ concerts. This was nice. We would have dinner after at the Gloucester House restaurant right on the water. It would be my mother, Jean, and myself. That's a really nice memory.

I was always forbidden to use the organ at home. It was too expensive, I was told. When home during the summer vacation I would wait for everybody to go to work and I would use it. Within months my playing was flawless. Being queer and mildly savant, I could play by ear and I picked up all the show tunes and Christmas carols. One Christmas I started playing. Jean nearly passed out. She seemed mad at first that I had snuck playing it when nobody was home, but got over that quickly and my playing was a total hit. To this day I can sit down at a piano or organ and the music will flow! My early Christmas holidays were okay. I remember the music, Bing and Nat, the snow, and some warm memories, but it turned ugly later as I grew older.

It was at Sunday school one morning that I realized what I had seen on that beautiful moonlit evening on Vine St in Saugus when I was five and a half years old. The teacher was showing us a picture of Jesus and explaining his love and devotion for people. I froze. But I told nobody. I kept it to myself as long as I could. It was my secret. And even if I told people about it, who would believe me? I can remember Sunday afternoon movies and I was always fascinated by "The Miracle of our Lady of Fatima" where the three children witness the appearance of the Blessed Mother in Fatima, Portugal in 1917. Even today, I still love that movie. I am planning a visit to Fatima sometime soon.

– CHAPTER THREE –

OFF TO JADE'S

We moved from my sister and Hank's house to a small apartment in Georgetown. We were constantly going back and forth. My mother and Jean would get into a fight and we would move out and they would make up and we would move back in. I always hated when we moved back. The fraught atmosphere was never ending in that house. Always negative turmoil. I loved it when we moved out. We lived in different apartments. One apartment that we lived in was a two-room woodshed art studio connected to the back of a house that belonged to a friend of my mother's. We fixed it up nicely. The lady's name was Jade. She was a lovely woman my mother's age and an avid artist in her spare time. Her watercolors were gorgeous. Some were a little off-color, so to speak, but beautiful. She was so ahead of her time. She reminded me of Rosalind Russell in Auntie Mame. The studio had a side bedroom that was small. My mother and I shared it with two small twin beds. The bathroom only had a walk-in shower but was fine for us; a small kitchen was part of the living room. The studio did have a little side brick patio that was nice. My mother worked two jobs to make ends meet. One was a secretary in Boston and the other was cleaning houses. I would make us dinner before she came home from the Boston job. Things were tight though. One of my specialties was sloppy joes on white hamburger rolls and mom loved it. I would make a small coleslaw too. I really gained some cooking skills through these years! Jade was so kind to us both. The rent was $50.00 a month. Not much, but my mother only made $75.00 a week with both jobs. Imagine that today. We stayed at Jade's for about a year. While there, however, Jade suggested to my mother that I see a psychiatrist to heal my gayness. She said a doctor might be able to reverse my odd feminine behavior. My mother took her suggestion and I went to visit a shrink in Beverly, MA. I went twice. It was a total waste of time and money. Wow, back then in 1968 people were so crazy. I knew why I was going and acted even extra feminine while talking to the doctor. His diagnosis was that I was a completely hopeless case and could not be medically helped or my condition reversed. He stated I was too far gone and I was destined to be a full-fledged homosexual. So we moved out of Jades and again we moved back to Jean and Hank's hell house. They were having money problems and my mother sucked it up and back we went. I always dreaded it.

My mother and I had wonderful summer vacations in Ogunquit, Maine. Money was always tight but she managed to get us up there for long weekends, overnights, and sometimes just for the day for a picnic on the beach. We always used to go out for a nice dinner in Ogunquit. My mother loved The Dancing Fan. It overlooked Perkins Cove and was a lovely spot. It was a little expensive so it was always a real treat to dine there. But again, things were not always sweet even when we lived at Jade's. A neighbor gave us a new kitten. I was happy but things were tight, and it was another mouth to feed, and the cat missed the litter box one day and pooped on the floor. My mother became furious. She said the cat had to go. I thought she was going to return it to the neighbor. Oh no. We both got into the car and the cat too and my mother chose a wooded road and put the cat in a paper bag. She stopped the car and threw the bag out the window into the woods. I can still remember seeing it slowly come out of the bag and look around helplessly. I was so sad. I asked my mother, "Will the kitty be okay?" She said, "Oh yeah…fine." I asked how it would eat. She replied that it will find something. How horrible is that? I never forgot that day. I have a beautiful cat today that I adore and spoil. Her name is Della and she is well taken care of and loved so much!

I attended Georgetown Public Schools all twelve years. First grade through the sixth grade were uneventful. Seventh grade was another story. I was obviously gay and could not hide it. It was 1968 and being gay was out of the question. I was labeled a freak queer. Again, the bullying was relentless and began the moment I entered the school and did not end until the end of the school day when I left. Every minute and every hour. Then after a full day of torture at school I rode the school bus home (more bullying) and then into Jean and Hank's hell house. When I waited for the school bus ride in the morning, sometimes Jean would be home and would yell out the window, "Davie!!! Got your yellow socks on Queerie!!" I had a pair of golden yellow socks that I thought were pretty cool. I would want to crawl somewhere and die. She did it to torment me, knowing the other kids would laugh. And she did it a lot. Jean had a major mean streak and could be outright cruel. The other kids didn't laugh. They actually laughed at her. She was so bipolar and so cruel and again I had no safe haven and I was helpless. My mother worked a lot; she needed the money. During the high school years, I had few friends. Not many would be seen with a queer. It was unheard of back in the early seventies. I was left alone and had only myself as my friend. Some of the teachers were nice, some were not. Some of the teachers didn't like queers either. I knew which ones they were. There was a reading teacher that was devoted to me though. She was very kind, caring, and made sure I could read and write properly. She would devote her lunchtime to tutor me. She was wonderful. There was the school librarian who was so kind to me as well. Then there was an English teacher that horribly berated me in class one day. I never really laughed in school because it was so bad and I was always sad. I was always down. This one day I was talking in her class and laughed at something. She scolded me right then and there in front of thirty other students and said, "Williams!! What's so funny? Be quiet or I am gonna wrap your skirt right around your neck!!!" The "skirt" part is that she knew I was gay and knew that would get to me. It did. I hushed up immediately while the other students snickered. I lost respect for her at that very moment and knew she was not a friend. It made me sad because I thought she was nice…strict but nice. That was in 1969. Today, she would at the very least lose her job. Not back then. Things were different. She wasn't the only teacher. I recall another male teacher used to play a game in class. He would blurt out a student's name and the other kids would quickly say what they thought. Like a pretty girl's name and the guys would yell, "Hot!!" He mentioned my name and most of the kids yelled out, "Queer!" I wanted to crawl under my seat. He knew that would happen. Another teacher had a group discussion in class about gay people. He spoke in such a demeaning way about gays. It was 1969 and the Stonewall NYC riots had just happened and he was looking at me as he spoke about gays and gay life. It was torture. I skipped Gym a lot because I was intensely bullied there. One day I was held down while a bunch of boys spat in my face and the other boys were punching my head. I would hide out in the library and help out there too. I felt safe there. The gym teacher never reported me because he knew the extent of the bullying, but never really addressed it. It was 1969 and it was totally allowed. In my high school years my mother struggled with money. Never had enough. She took up selling Avon beauty products on the side. I would go to neighbors' houses after school, selling it for her. A neighbor called my mother one day to place an order and said she had taken the book from me to order from and suggested to my mother that it probably wasn't a good idea to have me do that. I was already being over-bullied at school and if kids found that out it would be worse. Also, she mentioned that I had also put on way too much makeup myself as I sold door to door fully made up. I was a mess! But it was such fun. At sixteen I got my license but drove when I was fourteen. My mother would let me drive her around. I never got stopped though. The car was a 1965 Chevy Impala. Powder blue. What a classic. I remember when I was fifteen or so but did have my license yet my mother was ill. I drove her to Hale Hospital in Haverhill, MA. She was very ill and they kept her. This time I had to drive home by myself without her in the car. I was nervous and excited too. I can remember her saying, "Take the back roads home. Don't go to the main road." I did what she said. I was fine. I was glad a year later though when I could legally drive. Funny, today I do not drive. I haven't driven a car in close to forty years. I let my husband drive. I drive with my mouth. I can be a major backseat driver sometimes. I think I might like to get my license. Hey, it's never too late.

Graduation couldn't come quick enough. The day of graduation, I was so proud of myself for making it through six years of hell. It was a beautiful summer day and the graduation ceremony was outside. When my name was called, I walked up to receive my diploma and there was applause, but my hearing is good and I heard, "congratulations queer boy!" I was taken aback a bit but had a forcefield wall of steel around me after six years of this crap. I ignored it and took my diploma. I still think of it today though. Wow…how ignorant. School was finally done and I wanted out. In my senior year, there was a class trip to Spain and Morocco. My mother saved up and I saved a little from part time jobs and I was able to take the trip. It was so exciting and wonderful. That reading teacher that tutored me went too. It was amazing and I never forgot how exciting traveling to a strange new place could be. The plane ride over the Atlantic. The cities and coastline of the Costa Del Sol in southern Spain were gorgeous. Morocco was so mysterious, and the smell of oranges and spices filled the air. The hydrofoil ride from Spain to Ceuta in Morocco was so mysterious. It was like being in a movie. The rock of Gibraltar was beautiful and so magnificent. The open-air bus ride from Ceuta to Tangiers was majorly exciting with the view of the Atlantic Ocean traveling right on the sand. The Kasbah in Tangiers was unforgettable. The snake charmers and the aroma of smokey incense filled the streets and mysterious narrow alleys. I even rode a camel in the desert! Just wonderful, but so odd compared to my hometown of Georgetown. It was 1974 and the Boeing 747 had just come out and I got to fly home on it. It was amazing. This trip was such a reward after six years of hellish bullying at school. To this day, I never go a day without thinking about at least one bullying incident that happened during those teenage years. I still have anxiety over it along with the horrible memories of living at Jean and Hank's house, and I suffer from anxiety, depression, and OCD from it even as an adult today.

– CHAPTER FOUR –

OFF TO BOSTON!

I was done with school. Thank Goodness. I was skittish about college from high school and decided I would think about it later and go right into the workforce. Big mistake. I never entered a college until I was forty-five years old when I took a three-month Paralegal Crash Course at Northeastern University in Boston. It was now June of 1974, and I landed a job almost immediately after high school. It was a major insurance company in Boston. It was a very entry level position and I made a very pathetic salary. But I was out of high school, NO bullying, and there with some nice people. But also some not so nice people. Just because I was out of high school did not mean the hatred of gays wasn't out there. It was 1974 and it most certainly was in full gear. And it's bad when it's in management. And it was. They don't say it but you know it. The dirty looks, the double standards, the glares. It goes on. I realized at eighteen I was in for a bumpy ride at that moment in my life and for many years to come. I hated working in that insurance company. I was bored and was a lousy worker. I had no interest but to just mingle with people I liked and do as little as I had to. My mother was very ill with diabetes at this point and had battled the disease for years. She lost her battle in June of 1975. She was sixty-four and I was nineteen and I was devastated. She was my only friend other than myself. Now what do I do?

After three and one-half years I left. I moved on to a small insurance agency still in Boston. I stayed six months and left. I was being sexually harassed by a married man who was a closeted gay; it's not like today. You kept your mouth shut or you'd be fired. I looked for a new job. I got one working at a small real estate company doing billing. Horrible people. Catty women who made fun of me behind my back. I barely lasted a week. I was going out a lot in Boston. I was living on Mission Hill with a couple of roommates. They were both nice and they were both gay. I was there during the blizzard of 1978. The house was a three family but a little shabby. I can remember the house shaking during the blizzard. It was so very scary. Boston had and has a good-sized gay community. I was going to bars though I did not drink any cocktails nor drugs. But I hooked up pretty much nightly with different guys. Had sex on a regular basis with many different men. I was finally having fun.

CHAPTER FIVE

OFF TO NEW YORK CITY…1978

I had a friend whom I met in Boston. He was a flight attendant who had moved to New York City. I kept in touch with him and he suggested I move to New York and find a job there. Now the real trouble began. I moved to New York in the summer of 1978. I moved in with him. He was from Thailand originally and was a super great guy. So generous and caring. He was living in a good-sized one-bedroom apartment in Jackson Heights, Queens and shared it with me for about three months. It was close to JFK where he flew out of. The area was a bit sketchy though. I was chased home one night by three neighborhood thugs. I just barely made it in the door. New York was rough in many ways, and I wasn't streetwise at that point, but learned quickly. I got a job working for a large insurance agency on William Street in lower Manhattan. The people were very nice. The owner was a sweet older man who was very generous. He even gave me an advance of $500.00 that I paid back weekly, and I made a pretty decent paycheck. It was New York and it was in the late seventies and jobs were plentiful. Working and living in New York is a lot different than just visiting there on a weekend. It's hectic. And it's very expensive. The people are rough but nice at the same time. They put up with no bullshit. A cab will run you right down if you cross a street with a green light. They play no games, and you learn quickly!

The insurance job ended after about six months and I went on to a more clerical position at a major toy company on Fifth Avenue. The manager was very confrontational and just plain trouble and I only lasted a day. I came in ten minutes late and she fired me on the spot. New York was a tough place and people were tough skinned as well. I needed to get tough too or get out of there, but I wanted to stay. After getting canned I went to the Chock Full o'Nuts coffee shop next door and thought out what the next plan was to be. I got a new job really quick, but this time it was a temp position with an agency at a major NYC bank right away. It was okay. It lasted a couple months. I then went on to a CPA firm in midtown. I stayed there for about three months. It was hard there because they expected me to do more intense accounting work with numbers. I was good though; my OCD was finally paying off. It worked out and my boss was nice and she was patient with my somewhat limited skills and had no problem teaching me. I had now moved out of my friend's apartment in Queens and was living in a very tiny studio apartment in Brooklyn. It was on Stratford Rd off of Church Avenue. It was nice, but the protection of a free stay with my friend was over. I needed to keep a job. I needed to pay for my apartment and eat. While living in New York I also found myself hanging out in really sleazy places like this particular theater on 8th Ave in midtown west near Broadway. It was a gorgeous vintage old theater that had sadly turned into a gay male adult porn theater. There were tons of men's rooms, balconies, dark corners, all cozy little hideaway holes for great sex. And back then in the late 70s, unprotected, unsafe sex as well. I frequented this gem many times, but little did I know that I was treading on very dangerous territory with the AIDS pandemic lurking just around the corner, and New York City was one of the top breeding grounds for this horrible nightmare of a disease.

New York City was tough but so addictive. The big city feel, the nightlife, and just the excitement of being there and living there. It was so different from Georgetown and even Boston. But it was expensive, and I wanted to live right in the middle of it all, but I could not afford it. I needed part time work. Going out one night I stumbled into a hell hole of a bar. It was on 8th Ave midtown not far from that gorgeous old porn theater. I noticed young guys like me hanging out with older successful-looking gentlemen. I was kind of intrigued with this. These guys were male prostitute hustlers and were making good money escorting these older guys. This particular bar was very sleazy though. I was possibly interested in doing this temporarily for some side cash, but not here. I connected and networked with a couple of the hustlers and befriended one particular nice guy. He told me of another place he went on weekend nights. It was across town on the Upper East side and was very swanky. You had to look good and be presentable to get in, my friend told me. I got directions and went one Saturday night. What a difference. More classy-looking hustlers and very rich older gents. I was cute and young at that time and I did not drink any alcohol and did no drugs whatsoever. This was a major plus on my side. The older gentlemen liked it that I was "clean" so to speak. Never drunk or high and more of a "next door boy" type. I was hooking up nightly. I was making some nice side cash too. I had my regulars and I had walk-in tricks as well. The regulars were not always dependable. The walk-ins filled in the gaps. I was making enough money to get a very small East Greenwich Village studio apt. The area was a little sketchy, but I was finally living in Manhattan. I never brought tricks back to my apartment. That was my space only and I only went to their place and sometimes hotels and sometimes adult movie arcade booths when they were in a hurry. Once I had sex in a men's room stall in Port Authority Bus Terminal. Another time I had sex in a men's room right off the subway platform in lower Manhattan. The platform cleared of all people and a man followed me into the men's room. Totally unprotected sex in a New York City subway bathroom! How scary is that? How dangerous with AIDS! But at the same time, so exciting! Today, I would never even think of doing that. How disgusting!

I made the most cash from the hotel tricks. They were usually older, closeted married men who were on business in New York for a day or two. Back then in the late 1970s there were no mobile phones yet, so it was tough connecting. I had a particular phone booth between my apartment and midtown on West 4th Street in the West Village that I had the number to and would give that number out to tricks. It was frustrating though when I was waiting for a call and someone was using the phone. I would sometimes pretend I was using it but push on the button so the call could come in. I was also frequenting the saunas in New York as well. This was for pleasure. There were three or four in NYC. All were fun. I would have sex all night long. Sometimes with a dozen guys just in one night. I would totally be spent by the time I left at five a.m. the next morning so I could get to my office job on time. One night I met a very handsome younger man at that fancy bar. He was looking for "some company" for a so-called friend of his. He said the "friend" was a famous celebrity visiting New York and discretion was a major factor in me meeting him. He said my "junk" had to be inspected first because the friend was very particular about who would be escorting him. I went with this guy to the restroom at this Swanky Upper East Side club and let him inspect my stuff at the urinal. He smiled and said he was sorry, but I didn't make the cut. I laugh when I think about this today.

I always wanted to go to the totally trendy Studio 54 but I could never get in. I tried numerous times but I never got picked. There was a door man who stood on a platform and picked who he wanted. The celebrities just went right in with no problem. I was trying to go in on weekend nights. I tried numerous times, but no luck until one night. I dressed up a bit funky and was young and looked good and smelled awesome. I got picked! I got in. I was nervous, but made my way in. I could hear the disco music blasting. I was so excited. I don't remember the door admission, but it was expensive for me, maybe $20.00. But I did not drink any booze, so I remember even a Coke or bottled water was like $10.00 or something like that, so it was an expensive night. I did see a couple celebrities dancing, but by themselves. I went out to the dance floor and danced by myself along with them. I can remember it was a Bee Gees song. Next song was from Sister Sledge and then Sylvester. What a fun night, never to be forgotten.

– CHAPTER SIX –

"A NICE GUY"

I met another guy one day at an arcade sex store in Times Square. He was in his mid-thirties and a nice guy and very handsome too. He lived in New York on lower Park Avenue. He really didn't pay me for services, but actually just gave me money and we had great sex and enjoyed each other's company. I stayed with him often for a few weeks after meeting him. I would make him dinner or he would take me out to dinner at fabulous Manhattan restaurants and I very much enjoyed his company. I would sometimes go out on his terrace in the morning but he always kept a close eye on me, I guess thinking I would jump off or something and then how would he explain that to anyone? I was always happy being with him and the thought never crossed my mind. This relationship was short lived though. I knew I was just there for the moment and he wanted to venture out for other guys. He didn't want to settle down with a part time street hustler. He wanted more of a classy gentleman. That was fine and I moved on. I still think about him now and then and how sweet and kind he was. My life in New York was getting crazy. I was all over the place.

Now, you may ask, If you saw an apparition of Jesus as a child, then why on Earth are you prancing around New York City as a male prostitute? Good question. My self-esteem from my childhood was in the gutter.

When I dated or escorted these men, they temporarily adored me. They made me feel mighty good. They made me feel worthy, not worthless, and this was my addiction, not booze or drugs. I needed love and attention even as temporary or fake as it was. I needed it and absorbed every drop I could get! These men raised my self-esteem to a spectacular high. I loved it and loved myself and I ate it all up. And for the first time in years I knew I deserved it (and not to mention the extra cash that I truly needed to survive in Manhattan). Not a day goes by that I don't ask for forgiveness for these wrongdoings. And in New York City, survival is tough and only for the fit, so again this part-time gig came in very handy.

On Sundays I would always attend a Christian revival service near Times Square. It was in a parking lot on the corner of 42nd Street and Eighth Avenue, directly across the street from Port Authority Bus Terminal. It would take nearly an hour to set everything up. They had a huge Hammond organ that would be connected to a generator. It was amazing. The choral singers would next arrive and then the organist would start. Then the Pastor came. The service lasted two solid hours. I would always stay and was thrilled to be there. After the service there was tons of free coffee and donuts and I got to mingle with the singers and have my breakfast too!

I was going out more and more for nighttime fun. The meatpacking district was not what it is today. Today it's filled with trendy clubs, condos, and restaurants. Back in the late 70s it was dangerous. Smelly, oily streets from meat deliveries, tons of wholesale meat markets. There was a smell in the air that I can still remember today. Kind of musky and sweet and on a hot summer night it was very intense. There were dark streets and underground bars. There was one particular bar that was nicknamed the "Sleaze Pit." The Sleaze Pit was a sketchy underground leather bar that was so much fun. Hot and handsome looking guys and awesome back-room sex. You could smell the weed and leather the moment you entered. Major fun night spot. But again, very dangerous. Rest assured most of those guys contracted AIDS. Nothing short of a miracle if you didn't. I used to also go to the Chelsea Piers on the Hudson River to cruise for guys before they got trendy. They were deserted warehouses right on the West End Highway on the Hudson just there for the waiting. Enter at your own risk though. Very dangerous and especially at night. I sometimes went early in the evening and Sunday afternoons. A lot of fun! Tons of cruising and tons of very hot gay men. But again, I reiterate: dangerous AIDS territory. No condoms ever used. I cannot count the times I contracted Gonorrhea. I was a regular at the VD clinic on the lower east side medical walk-in. But never AIDS, which is impossible. I watched later as guys around me dropped like flies. Not me. Jesus has a purpose for me. We go back now to those twenty seconds in 1961. I have a job to do. To convey a message for love and devotion and peace that he seeks for this crazy planet called Earth. Especially now with this worldwide Covid pandemic. We need his help dearly.

– CHAPTER SEVEN –

DANGEROUS MOMENTS NYC

I lost my office job in New York. It was temporary and the assignment ended suddenly and I took to hustling full time until I could get another job. I had to eventually move out of my apartment and this was not good. I was making little money for New York standards and was basically on the street. I would rustle up enough cash to stay overnight at the bath house in lower Manhattan. They had small roomettes that were cheap, and I was safe off the streets, but very bad at the same time. I would sometimes meet guys at a bar and stay overnight with them but having sex was the price. I sometimes just wanted to sleep and relax in a soft bed, but it was a one-night stand and they wanted sex. But I got to stay overnight and it was free. I was at a Christopher Street West Village adult video arcade one day and noticed a poster on the wall that was soliciting good looking young guys to apply for "part time work" giving massages to guys and no experience was needed. I called the number and made an appointment to apply. They were two gay guys who lived in the West Village and the job was actually a call service. I would get a number to call and get picked up or go to their hotel or apartment. They were nice guys who ran the service, but they were actually pimps. I would give them 40% of what I made. I made good money though, even after paying them. And they had the connections, so it was less work for me to scout around looking for tricks. At this point, my life had turned into a mess. I was living in New York City as a full-time male prostitute on the streets. Could it get any worse? It does. One night I was on my way to the Club Baths about midnight. They had small roomettes for $20.00 for eight hours and I was going to stay the night. I was attacked as I entered by a homeless man. He beat me up and ripped my shirt off my back. I was screaming and the police showed up very quickly. They arrested him and put me in the back of the cruiser. They took him off in a patty wagon. They asked me where I lived and I replied "nowhere right now. I am just visiting Manhattan." I think they knew I was lying because I was actually homeless at the moment. They were so nice to me though. I never forgot that and to this day have always held the NYPD in the highest respect. They drove me from the lower east side into midtown. There was a homeless woman on the sidewalk around 23rd Street and Eighth Ave. She had a giant shopping cart filled with everything. The cops knew her. They said "Mona, you got anything this young man could get into…like a shirt?" Mona looked ragged, but at the moment she actually looked better than I did. She said, "Sure do Danny". She pulled out a long sleeve gray wool sweater. Mind you, it's mid-September and a heatwave as well and it's about midnight and it's still about ninety degrees out. But I got a sweater to cover up. I thanked Mona and the cops for their help and started walking. I had to find shelter but could not hustle that evening. I was a mess. I sighted a fleabag hotel up ahead near Ninth or Tenth Ave. The lobby was gross and the man at the desk looked disgusting. And then I realized the man was actually a woman and the lobby smelled like bleach and pine cleaner. I asked if she had any rooms available. She said nope. I was about to leave when this man that was standing behind me getting his key at the desk said, "Hey…you can stay in my room if you want." He was a younger-looking guy who looked like real trouble. Being desperate though, I took him up on his offer and went up with him. I was scared. He did bug me a little at first for sex but he was kind of high on something and quickly went to sleep. That didn't last long and he awakened and sat on the side of the bed and stuck himself with a syringe in his arm and shot up something. All of a sudden there was commotion outside our window. I got up to look, but the man I was sharing the room with said to keep clear of the window. I looked out and there were two men arguing and one had a gun. I got back into bed and was waiting to hear shots. I never did and I knew at this very moment that I was at the lowest of lows in my life. I would never be lower than this. I woke up early the next morning. I never slept a wink all night. I went into the bathroom to wash my face but there was no running water. What a dumpy hotel compared to the glitzy New York hotels I stayed in while escorting. The sun rose and I thanked the man for sharing his room and I was out the door. I made my way to Grand Central Station where I had locked up my belongings in a coin pay locker. I got all my stuff and took a quick shower at the "pay shower stalls" in Grand Central and headed to Penn Station for a train ride to Boston. I knew this was bad and I had hit rock bottom. I called my sister Jean and asked if I could come home. Jean and I had our moments along the years, but I must say she helped me get where I am. Without her help, I don't know where I would have ended up today.

— CHAPTER EIGHT —

NEW BEGINNINGS

I made my way to the Amtrak counter and explained that I had been robbed and needed to get home. They directed me to the "Traveler's Aid" counter. I was immediately assisted and Amtrak was so nice to me. Like the NYPD, I never forgot Amtrak and always use them when I travel to NYC to this day. I got a complimentary ticket directly to Boston. I went to my sister Jean's office. I never forgot the look on her face when I stood there. She started to cry and had to be taken out by a friend to the lady's room. She came back a few minutes later and we left for Georgetown. I felt completely lost. Back to this crazy house with Jean and Hank. No job. No money. No pride and no respect for myself. I was only back a few days when I got a job though. I started temping for Harvard University. I stayed for about six months. I moved on to Fidelity Financial. This job lasted five years. A milestone for me at this point. During these five years I moved into Boston again with a friend I had met temping (he has since died from AIDS). He had a great, small, but okay apartment in Boston's back bay. I went to the clubs on the weekend and kept myself busy during the week. Life was getting good. One Saturday I stumbled into a Gay owned coffee bistro in Boston's South End district. I met a man a little older, not much though, and we exchanged numbers. Well, I actually gave him mine. He didn't reciprocate. I thought something might be up but whatever. We hooked up about two weeks later. He was very handsome with very straight man qualities. They being very nice, very straight acting, very polite, no dissing, loved to eat, etc. I knew I was in love. This man and I have now been together for over forty years. The years were not all joy and rapture. We have had our ups and downs throughout those years. But who doesn't? Some turmoil and a lot of fun too. We finally legally married in Boston City Hall in 2017. Like I said, it has not been all joy and rapture. We lived for three years in a Boston South End apartment after living at my sister Jean's for six months. Those six months were turmoil. Jean was nice to let him stay there but there was always trouble. Not trouble like my childhood but just family turmoil. We ended up going away a lot on weekends up to Salisbury Beach. During the winter and summer and fall. Winter rates were dirt cheap and fun, with many times just relaxing at this particular cabin watching Channel 2 painting shows and picking apples in the fall and just chilling.

Just at the three-year mark we seemed to drift apart. I left and went back to my sisters for a bit and then got my own South End apartment with a girlfriend of one of the guys I was working with at a freight forwarding warehouse out at Logan Airport. I was doing accounting for them. The people were nice, and her boyfriend was a great guy. I hooked up with her and and we immediately became friends. She was a bit quirky, but a great person. The apartment was brand new, and we got along good. My ex-boyfriend was now living with someone else and at that time we were not really friendly. My new roommate was from California and I visited there three Christmases in a row. Much fun. Her parents were awesome. On my fourth visit it was to see her graduate from UCSB (University of California/Santa Barbara). She and I spent a weekend up to San Francisco. It was my first time there and we had a blast. She moved back to California, and I had a new roommate now. She was nice but only stayed a year. Then I had another roommate move in. His name was Bob. Nice guy but he smoked.

I got used to it. Bob and I lived together for the next four years. We were both gay but there was no romantic interest whatsoever, which is what I wanted. My ex-boyfriend was now back in the picture again. I ran into him one day and we rekindled our friendship. I was working at a major law firm in Boston and was laid off in 1991. I worked for an engineering firm in Cambridge for about six months. Shortly after Bob moved in with me in Boston's South End he stated he needed to go back to New Jersey to donate some bone marrow for his brother who was very ill with cancer. Bob came back much earlier than expected. He stated that he was unable to donate his bone marrow because of a childhood illness he had. I believed him but I kind of wondered if he was just saying that. I had a feeling something was up that he wasn't telling me. My sister Jean called me early one morning in September of 1990 shortly after Bob moved in with me and stated that Hank had passed away. It was a quick funeral and life went on. My sister never seemed the same though. With their horrific marriage and their dysfunctional relationship as bad as it was, my sister missed him dearly. Isn't life funny?

One winter in 1991 while living with Bob, I visited a friend named Jake who had moved to Florida. Jake had gone to the Orlando area and invited me to visit. He and his mother had bought a beautiful new home in the outskirts of Orlando. The town was created by a developer and it really was in the middle of nowhere. It was just swamp land. You had to be careful of alligators just walking. The house was small but was still quite lovely. Huge pool screened in and just a really nice setup. Jake took me to an outdoor gay men's retreat. There was a pool and clothing was optional. I actually had fun. We went directly there from the airport. We stayed the night and then went back to his house the next morning. His mother was quite ill and died a few weeks later. She was an older lady who was a lot of fun and drank too much. Another friend of his actually visited that same week. We all went to Key West for a couple days. It was an all-day drive from Orlando. But well worth it. Jake had booked us on a one-day cruise to the Dry Tortugas.

Great trip, but again it was clothing optional. I was not aware of this prior to the trip because yikes! It was not pretty! Not to mention it was a very hot sunny day. I came back with a nasty sunburn. All in all though, the trip was awesome. Sorry to say I never saw Jake again or that friend that visited that week also. They both died of AIDS shortly after this memorable trip.

― CHAPTER NINE ―

NEW YORK AGAIN! OH NO!!! 1992

I was out of work a couple of months after leaving the Cambridge engineering firm. Bob and I talked about moving to another city. We did. We moved to NYC in the spring of 1992. We rented a small Greenwich Village apartment in Chelsea and we were there only a few days when Bob suddenly became very ill. So I took him to St. Vincent's Hospital in the village. After a short workup in emergency, Bob was diagnosed with pneumonia. He had full blown AIDS. I had no job. Wow, here I go again!!! Well not really. I found a job pretty much right away. Bob was hospitalized for nearly a month. When he got out, he actually was ok. He also quickly found a job and we were doing okay. My ex came down one weekend, and we were doing good. As 1992 was ending, Bob became ill again. He went back to his mom's in January of 1993. I moved back to my sister Jean's house in Georgetown. I got a job in Boston and moved in shortly after that with my ex. That was over twenty-five years ago. We still live together today. We married at Boston City Hall in June of 2017. Through the years I have seen all of our dear friends and many acquaintances die of AIDS. This was especially true through the early 1980s and into the 90s. It seems every time I spoke to someone, they would say, "Oh, such and such died." It was awful. I lost many dear friends who I had known for years. I, however, never contracted AIDS. Even after being totally promiscuous in Boston and New York City in the late 1970s, which was prime time to contract it. I never did. This I realized later in life was impossible. I realized this was a total divine intervention. Now we go back to 1961 on the night I saw Jesus walking for twenty seconds in the clouds. No AIDS for me. But why? Why, I ask, when so many wonderful people lost their lives? Not me. No real bad illness for me through the years either. I think I know why. I'm here for a purpose. But what? I have researched apparitions far and wide. Bottom line is an apparition is meant to benefit the holy figure giving it rather than the person receiving it. Which means Jesus wanted something. But what could I possibly offer? I'm still somewhat slow with mild savant syndrome and somewhat limited abilities. Then I started to put two and two together one evening when I woke up in the middle of the night. He wants me to write a damn book. He wants me to talk about the apparition. He wants me to share my crazy life and love and tell everyone I know and everyone I don't know. I'm doing it. Even with savant syndrome, there comes optimum memory far exceeding normal people, and an amazing tiny island of brilliancy in the brain. My writing skills are okay, too. They would not have been without the extra tutoring I got from my wonderful teacher back in high school. She was in the plan too. With her care and kindness, I managed to put a book together pretty well.

– CHAPTER TEN –

BACK HOME, 1994

I came back home from New York. Bob went to his mother's in Ohio. He wasn't doing well. I kept in touch but Bob was in denial and wasn't talkative. He couldn't understand how and why I had dodged the bullet with AIDS. He even said once I must have been "chosen." I told Bob about my apparition. He said that Jesus chooses certain people even before they are born to do a job for him. There is always a purpose. I initially stayed at Jean's house after returning home from NYC, then moved on to a couple I knew in Brookline, MA for a couple months, and then to my ex's apartment in the Fenway section of Boston. I was only going to stay six months with him, but I never did leave. I moved in with him on New Year's Day 1995. We went to San Francisco that summer for a week. It was my second visit there and it was very fun. Bob called me from Ohio that Labor Day weekend and I met him in Boston. He was in Boston for a few days visiting and had some medical appointments. He was staying with a friend of his from where he used to work. I met him at a Starbucks downtown. I had not seen him in three years and was devastated when I laid eyes on him. He was no more than one hundred pounds. His face was completely gaunt. I was shocked. AIDS had totally eaten him away. That was September. Bob died the next month, and I was very upset even though I knew it would be soon. Bob had a lot of personality issues and really wasn't liked but I knew he had a good heart and didn't deserve this. I looked back at my spicy dicey past in NYC and looked up some old friends. All dead from AIDS. None survived. It was beyond sad. Some of them were funny, campy old queens. Some were very handsome men. But all were nice. And none of them deserved suffering and ultimately death. Beyond sad.

I got a job at a small law office in Boston specializing in third-party collections. I stayed there for six years. They were nice people but I needed to move on. My ex and I moved to Dorchester in 2000 because the Fenway apartment was too small. We got a good-sized condo that he bought and we stayed there for five years. In 2000 I landed a job for a boutique-sized Boston law firm which I worked for until 2020. Twenty solid years…a milestone for me! We moved to the Ashmont section of Dorchester in 2005. This place is gorgeous. We are still there. The job was awesome and the people were my family. My ex worked there for fourteen years and retired in 2017. In 2013 I had risen to well over 300 pounds. I had already had a mini stroke and had gone into AFib irregular heartbeat twice because of sleep apnea. My doctor was furious with me. I finally gave in and had gastric bypass weight loss surgery. It had an amazing turnout for me. I lost 150 pounds and was actually healthy. No more sleep apnea and no further heart issues. But the surgery came with other problems. I started to drink a little more than I should have. The cocktails take effect very quickly and I try to watch it now more carefully.

– CHAPTER ELEVEN –

WHAT IS LOVE?

Love is a many splendid thing…or so they say. During my childhood there was not much of it out there for me. I grabbed what was offered but it was slim pickings. My mother did love me very much. The rest of my family, not really that much at all except my niece. She is my sister Carol's daughter who I still have a relationship with today. She lives north of Boston and we see each other on occasion but not enough.

So, when you don't receive love, you don't know how to give it. It takes a toll on friends and relationships going forward. Most people do not understand. Sometimes I feel I have so much love to give but it's hard to give it out. I rarely trust anyone and was always afraid of getting emotionally hurt. I am already a broken person, and I don't need any more anxiety or sadness in my life. My husband does truly love me unconditionally. It took me a long time to accept it though. Jesus loves me unconditionally too, and I realized this more than ever recently. Forgiveness comes with love hand in hand, and I forgive everyone for their wrongdoings to me. Or I at least try my best. I never hold a grudge because if you don't forgive, I have learned that you become a prisoner. It holds you back and it churns around in your mind and makes you hateful and resentful. Believe me, no one needs that. It's true what they say: You can never forget things but should always let go and forgive. Never hold on to it. I know this is easier said than done, but it's so true and I know this from experience. I have held grudges and hated people in my past. But I was the only one who really suffered. Jesus works in such mysterious ways. Things have turned around for me so many times because of faith in him. His mother asked at Fatima, Portugal in 1917 that that we pray and that we forgive and that we have faith in her son. This is a must if this world is going to survive. We need Jesus more than anything, especially now in this broken and bruised hell of a world.

— CHAPTER TWELVE —

WHAT IS COURAGE?

Courage is a big word. It takes courage to have courage. I know that sounds weird but it's so true. The bullying that I went through during my teens was abominable. When I think about it, I even wonder to this day how I managed to not commit suicide. Life then was horrible, and I felt so worthless and hopeless. I didn't have the courage to stand up for myself, but I built up the courage to not kill myself. I see and read sometimes about teenagers who kill themselves because of bullying in high school and at home. Back in the 1960s and 1970s, bullying was done in person. Today there is cyber bullying. I don't know which is worse. I think probably in person. They can get physical with you, which is against the law today. Not back then. I hated myself back then. I hated my life, I hated who I was, and I hated everyone around me. Life has taught me a major lesson to stand up for myself. I now love myself. I now have the courage to set people straight. I have the courage to be who I am and be proud of it and without any questions whatsoever.

— CHAPTER THIRTEEN —

POT OF GOLD

They say there's a pot of gold at the end of the rainbow. I think this is kind of true. But the pot of gold is not gold nor is it monetary. The pot of gold, so to speak, could be many things. It is not based on luck. The pot of gold I believe comes from Karma. What goes around comes around right back to you. Being nice, helping people, loving people unconditionally: this is how we each get our pot of gold. And we know when we get it. I received a giant pot of gold the night Jesus appeared to me on that moonlit evening. I never asked for that. I believe I was chosen long before I was born. I was chosen to receive the divine miracle of life. I should have died so long ago. But Jesus selected me to tell this story and I am. Many people may not believe this and that's fine. They may say I just want to make money from my memoir. Not true. I don't want or need the money. All proceeds from my book will go to help homeless people and animals in need. All to charity. Jesus would want that.

—CHAPTER FOURTEEN—

"TIME"

So much time went by from the time I saw the apparition of Jesus and the time it took to finally write my memoir and to convey his message of love and peace for the world. We need to take the time to love one another. To forgive those who have hurt us. To help those who really need our help and not just with money but with caring and talking and being there when someone needs us and not expecting anything in return. Over the years since that night, I have crossed so many paths I should not have. But I did, and Jesus guided me and helped me get where I am today. Like I have said so many times, I am lucky to be alive. And I am answering his wishes.

– CHAPTER FIFTEEN –

PEACE...

Peace is wonderful but comes with a price. Never underestimate how wonderful peace can be. Never take for granted how wonderful peace can be. The price is not monetary. The price is love. Love yourself and love your family and love your friends and show it and give it out. That can be hard sometimes. Love your neighbors and your co-workers. Many times, coworkers turn into family. Help someone in need. Help someone you don't even know. It would probably mean the world to them. I give $10.00 to a homeless man I see every Friday. He looks a little mental but wow, do I get a smile! That's a coffee and meal or even a nip of gin; I don't care how he spends it. I give it to him and it's his to do what he wants with it. When I was down and out in NYC years ago, I once met a stranger on the subway and we talked for a while. She knew I was in need. She handed me $5.00. Back then that was like $50.00. She simply handed it to me and smiled. I put it in my pocket and thanked her. Today I am financially stable and can help people by giving back. You have to give back. It brings you peace.

–CHAPTER SIXTEEN–

TRUST...

Trust is a touchy and complicated subject. Who can we trust? That's the question. Can we trust our friends? Can we trust our family? Can we trust our instinct? That's hard to say. I can trust most of my friends in my small circle. I think! My co-workers and boss? Some of them, but not all of them. I learned that the hard way. My niece and her family are the only blood family I can trust. Can I trust my instinct? I'm not sure. I have trusted people in the past that I thought were trustworthy and genuine and they didn't turn out to be. I didn't make a good judgment call and I got hurt. But that unfortunately is how we learn our lessons in life. I have learned many times and made the same mistake in trusting someone in my lifetime. And just when you think you are finished making mistakes, you make another one. I still do it today. I do know one thing for sure. I can trust Jesus. He is always there for me. Sometimes it takes a while and then Boom! He takes care of it. And sometimes in very strange ways. I am always amazed because he works so mysteriously. Sometimes the mystery scares me but always stuns and amazes me.

– CHAPTER SEVENTEEN –

MONEY...

Money, they say, is the root of all evil. Is it? We need it to eat. We need it to pay for our housing. We need it to travel. We need it for just about everything. So when does it become evil? And why? Money becomes evil when greed comes into play. When that happens people will do anything to get it. And it's never enough. When I was young and stupid, I thought I just wanted to be rich. I sometimes borrowed money and never paid it back. I thought the world owed me something. The world owes me nothing. I learned that all too well later in life. I never had enough. In NYC I even sold my body as a male prostitute as you have already read. Why was I even in New York? I knew I couldn't afford it. It's all about greed and envy. I could say, "WOW, I live in Manhattan. Whoopy!" I temporarily had plenty of money. Very temporarily kind of rich but not really. Why was I doing that? I thought I was a big shot. I was young, kind of good looking and wanted people to be jealous that I had a great life in New York. And I was greedy. When I would walk into a fabulous Manhattan restaurant that my very temporary boyfriend from Park Avenue brought me to, I would walk in like I owned the place. If it wasn't for him taking me, I couldn't even afford a toothpick in there. I was greedy and arrogant. I would order the most expensive thing on the menu. How sad is that? I was just a broken person who wanted to be someone I'm not. Today I am not like that. I realize how stupid it was and I am very rich today, richer than I ever could be. Not with money though. With love, caring, doing things that make me happy like cooking, going to my job, and gossiping with co-workers that I truly love as my family, getting up every morning and seeing the sun, enjoying the fall with long walks with my husband, grabbing a cocktail on the way home, going to church on Sundays and taking communion. Simply enjoying my life without being pretentious. At the end of the service at church the rector always says the whole set of the Lady of the Rosary Hail Mary. It always chokes me up. She loved her son so much. She loves everyone so much and deserves to be recognized. I see so much on Facebook about "loving your mom," even dead moms in heaven. We need to pray to Mary the lady of the Rosary. The world is in total turmoil. We need her more than anything right now. And she wants to help. Let's pray to her and help her to help us. We dearly need her help.

– CHAPTER EIGHTEEN –

ATHEISTS...

The meaning of an atheist I believe is the disbelief of God or Gods and any or all religions. In the Miracle of our Lady of Fatima movie, Hugo was the children's best friend. He made sure no one hurt the three children who witnessed the Holy Blessed Mother Mary's appearance. He also did not really believe they witnessed it. Hugo was an atheist but dearly loved the children. On the sixth month, which was the last visit from Mary in October of 1917 in Fatima, Portugal, he made sure the kids were there on time. She always appeared at noon. He made sure the 70,000 people that had pilgrimaged to the field where she appeared did not bother the children. The crowd was getting restless because they were waiting for a promised miracle by the blessed mother. She had promised to give one on her last visit in October. She kept her promise indeed. She raised her left arm towards the sky. The rain stopped and the sun, which was not out, slowly appeared. The sun came twirling towards the earth. People ran for their lives. People were frightened and amazed at the same time. Crippled people were healed, blind people could see. The soaking wet, muddy field turned dry. The sun stopped twirling and Hugo could be seen looking shocked. He then states in the movie, "Only the fools don't believe." Hugo is right. He witnessed something that day that changed his mind instantly. Hugo's soul was saved. This was another miracle that day. I myself witnessed an appearance from Jesus on the night when I was six years old, and this was totally a mystical gift for me.

– CHAPTER NINETEEN –

FREEDOM...

They say we have the freedom to be what or who we want to be. Do we? Do we without ridicule or prejudice? Without people glaring at us? Without them laughing at you? What gives anyone any right to judge anyone? And to hurt people that don't act or be like they think we should be? This is where freedom comes into play. When you start to not act the way you want or be who you want to be, your freedom is compromised. Why do we do this? Perhaps for family or your job. Or out of embarrassment. It doesn't matter that the freedom is gone. This becomes sadder as we get older. Your life becomes a lie. I am a gay man who never had the ability to hide it. I just didn't. I was always queer and looked and acted it. I used to be ashamed. No more; that ended years ago. I don't care what people think. I never did but I found myself trying to hide it for various reasons that I don't give a crap about anymore. I learned to love myself. It took years though. I actually hated myself at one time. No more. I love me. I love people. I love animals. I love to love and be loved. I learned this and am so grateful to have been able to learn this. Some people never do. They go to their graves hateful and never loved. They lose their freedom. I'm not going to do it. These people had no faith and no reason to change. I know this for a fact: some of these people were my family.

– CHAPTER TWENTY –

POST-TRAUMATIC STRESS DISORDER AND DEPRESSION (PTSD)

PTSD is a horrible thing. It causes major anxiety, depression, stress, addiction, OCD, anger, and fear; the list goes on and on. I have it and I have had all the symptoms mentioned here. It takes over your life if you let it. It's easy to give in though. And it's sneaky how it works too. I've learned how to fight it. But it never all goes away. There are tell-tale signs that are always there. In my opinion, there really is no treatment. Depression can be treated with medication, but it can be addictive. You can try to learn to live with it but it's hard. Years of abuse and intense bullying caused this, and it remains with me until I die. Unless you face it straight forward and fight it. Really quite sad. Learning to love and forgive the people that did this to me is the only way I get relief. But that's very tough. You need to have a clear head for this and follow it through. As always, love prevails and true faith in Jesus that he will never forsake you and be by your side until the end. Never ever give up on him. I know that from true experience.

– CHAPTER TWENTY ONE –

THE GIFT...

The gift is mine and mine to keep. It was the apparition of Jesus at six years old. I have seen him and know he exists. The event that night was surreal at the very least. The silver puffy clouds with the full moon shining and his bright image walking ever so slowly. Most people will never get this gift. Some believe and some don't. I care, but I don't care. Some people will always be skeptical. That's just peoples' nature. It is amazing when something like this happens to you; it opens your eyes. Every day I count my blessings that I experienced it. I want to share that gift with everyone. It really happened. Jesus exists. He most definitely does. He loves us and wants us to believe that he is there for everyone. Please share my gift along with me.

– CHAPTER TWENTY TWO –

COVID-19 - CORONAVIRUS - THE YEAR...2020

The year is 2020. It starts off okay. The weather in New England is mild with no real big snowstorms. Economy is awesome. Things look good. Mid-January I got ill with something. I rarely go to the hospital with cold or flu symptoms because I very rarely get ill. This thing was different. I felt sick. No fever or chills, but really nasty chesty respiratory symptoms with a slight cough. I could breathe fine, but my diabetes, which went into remission after my weight loss surgery, was totally out of whack. My blood sugar numbers were spiking so I decided to make the trek into the city to my doctor's office, which is in a major Boston Hospital. My primary care doctor was not available because she was booked so another doctor saw me. She took one look at me and put on a mask. I already had one on and because I assumed I had a cold when I checked in, so the front desk gave me one. She examined me and corrected me when I said I had a cold. She stated firmly, "You have some kind of a flu." She made a very firm suggestion that I return home and get into bed and stay out of work for the rest of the week and provided me with a doctor's note. It was Tuesday. I took her suggestion and recovered nicely. My husband also became sick, but not as bad as I was. He recovered also. Did we have the Coronavirus? I don't know. I believe we did. The state ordered in late March all non-essential offices be closed. My office closed and I needed to work from home. My husband is retired so it's been weeks and I am still at home. We have tried to not get on each other's nerves, but that is hard. We eat and drink more than we should. But that's actually the fun part.

I read something online where people who are sick of being quarantined asked when can we get back to normal? The short answer is we can't ever get back to normal. Normal wasn't working. Many people are selfish and nasty and quite greedy. We need to be more kind, loving and helpful to others. Do not gossip and make fun of people's shortcomings. I'm guilty as well. I'm no better than many people. I've done my share of sometimes belittling people to make myself seem or look better. This time away has given me and a lot of people the time to think. I had time to think about how I was bullied in school and at home in my childhood. I thought of the cruelty I was subject to. It's time for everyone to love one another and worry about one another and help one another. It's not hard to see that Jesus is offended by peoples' actions. Did he create this virus? I don't know. But if he did, what a genius. It stopped people in their tracks. It gave people time to think like myself and to make changes in their life. To slow down and take the time to smell the roses. I never knew what that meant. I do now.

– CHAPTER TWENTY THREE –

MY SISTER JEAN

As I have told some chapters back, my sister Jean helped me very much during my life when she was alive. I got myself into situations where I needed help to come back to her home. I needed someone to talk to. I needed guidance and understanding, and she was always there to give It and it was not always what I wanted to hear, but she was old-school and doled it out and not sugar coated either! She came through and helped me as much as she could through my crazy years in and out of NYC and pulled me out of the gutter more than once or twice for that matter. Crazy boyfriend situations. Crazy rescues in the middle of the night. You name it, she was there for me. My earlier days and early teens were sketchy with her. She definitely had a mean streak and was hot and cold in many situations. There was definitely verbal and emotional abuse involved. Back in the 1960s and 1970s, I think it was more of a norm than it is today. I sadly got used to it happening. Like I mentioned a few chapters back, Jean had a rough childhood. She was bitter and cold. She tolerated my mother somewhat and tolerated me for the most part. My childhood was much better than hers. She knew that. But it wasn't my fault. But down deep, Jean was caring and kind. She would help a stranger in a heartbeat in any way she could. But you really had to dig to get it. There was no hugging or kissing that I can remember on any occasion and very few kind words. She mellowed out in her older years. We got along better, and she leveled off to being a fairly nice person but never really happy. We enjoyed going to lunch together and reminiscing about old times. I often thought to myself that Jean was bi-polar and still think she was. Her mood swings were too sudden, and you never knew what was coming and neither did she. When she died, a part of me also died. I loved Jean and I still miss her very much, as crazy as it was. She was like a mother to me. She is always included in my bedtime prayers to Jesus that she is happy and being watched over. She deserves it. Jesus knows that too.

– CHAPTER TWENTY FOUR –

MY MOTHER DOROTHY

My mother was an interesting woman. Yes, she abandoned a cat. I know. But some people back then did bad things like that. Like the neighbor who watched me in the afternoon after school. The family lived down the street from us in Georgetown. The family cat had kittens and they had no money to feed them. The father drowned them all in the nearby brook. Terrible. My mother worked three jobs to put food on the table and would make sure I had nice clothes and a giant Easter basket on the kitchen table on Easter morning. And Christmas presents under the tree were plentiful. We went to Church on Christmas Eve and most Sundays. She did the best she could and at the time I took it for granted. Things were tough back then in the 1950s and the 1960s and 1970s. It's not anything like today, but I am glad I lived in that era. It's not as great today as everyone might think. It's a tough world out there. I'm glad I had the experience of living back then to temper myself in today's world. People were much different back then. Somehow somewhat nicer and caring. Today's world is very fast and very complicated. My mother was born in 1911 so she saw everchanging times. She lived through the 1918 Spanish Flu, the depression of 1929, and she dated men in the 1940s. She was a well-seasoned woman. She was kind in her own way, but a tough cookie and not to mention a horrible cook. She could barely boil water. We prayed she didn't cook so we wouldn't have to eat it! She attempted numerous times to help me out with the intense bullying, but to no avail. It never got better until I was out of high school for good. She was a good, protective mother who, again I reiterate, did the best she could. And I respect and will always love her dearly for that. I know Jesus knows all this. She is in his hands now.

– CHAPTER TWENTY FIVE –

MY SISTER CAROL

My sister Carol was a wonderful lady. She certainly had her shortcomings as a mother. But she tried the best she could. As she aged, she was a better mother and a wonderful grandmother. She was judged by many as an unfit mother, including my mother. This was in part for marrying a man and leading a single woman's life with him, dragging my niece across the country working in a traveling carnival. They ended up homeless in Florida and my mother and Jean had to pull them out of the gutter. My mother judged them, but people sometimes forget that my mother deserted Jean at an early age to work in Florida in a cushy job hanging around rich men. She was a good mother to me for the most part, but could've easily been judged as an unfit mother to Jean. Wow, then I run off to NYC to start a new life and end up as a male prostitute. I guess the apple doesn't fall far from the tree as the old saying goes. I do however remember as a child my sister Carol being very nice to me and a lovely person. When we all lived in Lynn I remember beautiful long walks to my mother's best friend that we called Auntie Gizzy. She had a gorgeous big home with a huge wraparound front porch directly on Lynn Beach, right on the Lynn Shore Drive. In those days they called those homes "white elephants"; gigantic homes for cheap. No one wanted them. Too much to heat and take care of. Today it still stands but was made into four condos. That's how huge it was. Carol sadly died way too early at fifty-nine from complications from diabetes. I still love and miss her.

CHAPTER TWENTY SIX

MY BROTHER-IN-LAW HANK

This, as they say, is a horse of a different color. Hank was born in 1921. He lived in Saugus where my sister met him. My sister had already been married twice to the same man. I know…huh? But yes. Hank was forty-one when my sister married him. Never before married and set in his ways. Hank never made it past the third grade. His parents pulled him out of school to work on their farm. It was a huge pig farm in Peabody about fifteen minutes north of Saugus. Back in the depression days of 1929, parents were allowed to pull their kids out of school, which today is illegal. He never went back to complete his education and could barely read or write and it was sad. My sister knew this but married him anyway with no education and he was also very bipolar. He was actually in a mental hospital in Western Massachusetts, about two weeks prior to Jean marrying him. He had a nervous breakdown because his mother, who was the matriarch of the family, had suddenly died of a massive heart attack. He was stricken by this and never really did recover. Under his tough and very brutally mean streak was actually a very kind man. My sister unfortunately was the gasoline for his fire though. She could set him off in a second and we all would suffer. His profane, crazy outbursts were horrifying, and no one would be spared. He never really had a job for more than a few weeks and made very little money. The $50,000.00 he inherited when my sister married was blown right through within months. Then that was it. And she knew it. She married him anyway and lived a hellish life for the next twenty-five years. I can remember him being so nice and then turning on a dime to spit out the worst remarks and get physically abusive. My sister finally had him put in a residential care facility in 1988 but he committed suicide one evening. My sister never really got over it. He died a very unhappy man and that's the sad part. I can't say I miss him, but I always think of him and pray to Jesus to comfort and take care of this poor soul.

— CHAPTER TWENTY SEVEN —

2020 RACIAL RIOTS

With the COVID-19 pandemic still lurking in our midst, we now have been thrown right into the mixing bowl, another huge problem. Not as big as the virus problem itself, but just as important in another way. It's a buildup of blatant racial discrimination. The issue at hand is major police discrimination and brutality. A man who died at the hands of police officers on duty. A police officer who dug his knee into a black man's neck for nearly nine minutes while he cried out and begged for mercy and cried out numerous times that he could not breathe. This man died of a heart attack and asphyxiation per the autopsy. This is disgraceful and not to mention unheard of. And now with the tensions of the pandemic, we have the tensions of the protesting. People do need to stand up for their rights because black lives do matter. But in Jesus's eyes, everyone's life matters. Yes…everyone! We all matter. I wish I could have protested when I was being massively bullied as a teenager for being a homosexual. Not a chance. The protests for gays were not until the 1969 Stone Wall riots. I wish I could have protested for the times I was fired for being gay. It was done so sneakily but right in my face. Blatant, overt discrimination. Very subtle and passive, but I still got canned. I had to find another job right away. Bills to pay, rent to pay, food to buy. You can't go too long. You know when the firing is coming close too. Your boss does not like gays: the looks, the remarks, the extra work when you already have enough. I can be a little slow too. Perfect excuse to get rid of me. Happened a number of times. The seventies and mid eighties were bad for that crap. Things seem to be a little better today, but are they really?

– CHAPTER TWENTY EIGHT –

LIFE GOES ON!

Life continues to go on even during the COVID-19 Virus. I am having problems working from home. I cannot be as efficient as I am at work. For that reason, I go in. It's about a twenty-minute trek from my apartment in Dorchester to downtown Boston's financial district. I wear my mask and try to stay safe. Downtown Boston is still very eerie. Not many workers are going to work. The trains are dead. It's a little eerie and quite pleasant at the same time. I always get a seat and it's quiet on the subway. Not many going to work so it makes it nice, but lonely at the same time. I actually get excited when a coworker comes in that I have not seen in a while, at least the ones I like. I do miss my coworkers and the fun though and the gossip but all in all it's okay. All in good time they say. Some coffee shops have opened near my apartment and I go to the small shops that need the money and tip extra. These poor people have struggled through this pandemic and are hungry for just a customer. The restaurants in Boston are also struggling. I sometimes would bring my breakfast, but not always, and always buy my lunch. There are places, you just have to sniff them out. The weekends are boring. Brunch maybe. Who knows who's open this week? A walk or a stroll to the convenience store for a lotto ticket. That's about it. Nothing going on. But the one thing that is going on is eyes get opened. We look around in disbelief. Downtown Boston is not bustling like it usually is. The financial district is eerily dead. I go into work almost full time now. Working from home can be very challenging for everyone in the workforce. I like being in the office with all my familiar surroundings, and everything runs smoother. I have a new boss too. My former boss was there for seventeen years and was so sweet and understanding. This one is also very sweet. I was sometimes expected to do things that are out of my comfort level. But I have had to take on new tasks that I did not think I could handle, but I do, and I try my best. Sometimes you do not think you can do something when you really can, and all in all do well and perform the best I can and do a good job.

– CHAPTER TWENTY NINE –

FINALLY FINDING COMPASSION

I was let go from my law firm position after twenty-plus years. No surprise really. I knew it was coming. A lot of changes at the firm between the pandemic and new management and budget issues. I was gone along with others. I got a new job working for a larger law firm, but it only lasted eight weeks. Another one bites the dust! Horrible position and I was not happy. After leaving the larger law firm, I looked into something totally different. No more law firms. I applied for a department coordinator position for a large hospital in the greater Boston area. I got the job. This job, unlike the accounting positions at the law firms, requires me to be compassionate. This was a definite requirement. Kindness was also a major requirement. You are helping people of all ages and who are all different in their wants and needs. They depend on you to be there and to be kind and understanding of their needs. I am there for them. My boss is a dream boss. She is just perfect, and I have never been happier in a job than this one. I know now that this was a divine intervention. I was losing control in the other jobs I had. I was getting hateful and not happy. Jesus guided me and helped me get this job. Working here has helped me to feel total compassion for people. To care for them and help them in ways I could not have imagined a couple years ago. I love my job. I look forward to going in every day. The doctors and nurses are so nice. I have certainly come miles since my earlier days. They say the last chapters in your life are better than the first chapters. This is so true. I love people and want to be loved. The Omicron virus strain is now upon us. I hear it's not as deadly and especially if you are vaccinated. But some people don't want to be vaccinated. My job and my workplace are very busy. I want to help as much as I possibly can.

Something odd has been happening for the last six months or so. I started waking up at night at exactly 1:11 am and 2:22 am and 3:33 am and out of the shower at 4:44, arriving at work at 5:55 am. This has been happening for about six months or so. I found it odd because it was happening so much, so I googled it. These are angel messenger numbers, offering care and help and encouragement. The 1:11 am sign I get is really interesting. It states the angels are saying that a looming decision needs to be taken care of. This signal is my book publishing. I seem to be a procrastinator. And the pandemic has taken its toll. I am very busy at work and had to fit in finishing this book. But the 1:11 am number message states not to worry and to focus and move forward. You are reading my book now. I have taken the advice.

– CHAPTER THIRTY –

BULLYING

Bullying is a sensitive subject for me. I was bullied at home during my early childhood and my teenage years. I was also bullied at school in my teenage years and it continued up to just recently when I got fired from my job of twenty-plus years working for a Boston law firm. Bullying is horrible. I have a passive personality, so I can be easily bullied, and I don't usually fight back. I do have a limit though and it can be reached with speed if people go too far. To be bullied on a daily basis is nerve-wracking. It is tiring and leaves you also on edge because you never know what's around the corner. It leaves you feeling hopeless and worthless and it gnaws on your spirit. You lose respect for yourself when you don't stick up for yourself. Bullying continued after high school in the workforce. It's just a little different. And it's not only bosses that do the bullying. It can be co-workers as well. I'm older now and more street-wise, meaning I can defend myself for the most part, but it still disturbs my spirit when it happens. I try to get along with everyone but with some it takes extra energy to do it, but you have to try hard and make it work. Being kind and happy can set the tone for the bully. They don't like it and it's a perfect way to react to their actions. It catches them off-guard and they get embarrassed, especially with other nice people around. Today in the year 2020, it's actually not different than back in 1970. Bullying still happens and will always happen. The key is in how you handle it. The bully needs to be set straight right from the start. Always remember that they are the idiots…not you. And never lose respect for yourself. When you do, it shows and they feed on it. And never let your guard down. They will take any advantage to step right in. And again, always love yourself.

– CHAPTER THIRTY ONE –

THE END OF MY STORY...I SURVIVED!

This has been my story. This book is labeled a short story or a parable or maybe just a long letter. It is a kind of a short story that tells a lot in a small amount of time. It is a condensed synopsis of my life from 1956 through the beginning of 2022. I wrote the best stuff and left out the boring stuff. I know some things can be confusing. First, I met my husband in 1981. We have known each other since then. We did however breakup in 1984. He went his way and I went mine. We did not connect back as friends until 1988. We rekindled our friendship then and remained friends until today. I moved in with him in 1995 and have been living with him for the last twenty-six years. We legally and officially married in 2017. My friend Bob who I went to NYC with in 1992 was just a roommate who I met through an ad I put in the local gay Boston newspaper for my spare bedroom in an apartment in the south end of Boston at that time, which was 1988. We did become friends though as years went on. As you remember, poor Bob died of AIDS in 1995. Our last six months as roommates ended in NYC in January of 1993. He went home to Ohio, and I moved home to my sister Jeans in Georgetown in Northern Massachusetts. Bob did come back to Boston to visit some friends in September of 1995. We met for lunch and shopped a little bit. He died the next month.

Let me please be clear. I did indeed see the image of Jesus in the clouds that evening back in 1961. Why this happened puzzled me for years. I know some people will be skeptical and will never believe me, and that is fine. I have no reason whatsoever to make it up. But it did happen and has had an effect on the changes during my lifetime. When I lived in NYC during the AIDS pandemic, let me reiterate again that I had unprotected sex with hundreds and hundreds of men. I know there is no way whatsoever I could have dodged that bullet. Not a chance. This was truly a miracle. Later in life, I somehow realized that. It hit me one night and I knew my service to Jesus was to tell this story and write a book. He wants people to know I saw him and to believe he truly exists. He radiates nothing but pure love for all mankind. This appearance was truly a GIFT!

Let me say thank you to the many people who kept me inspired and supplied me the energy to write and complete this book. This includes my husband and numerous friends. A very special thank you to a special lady whom I worked with at the law firm I was let go from. She is a pastor as well as a legal assistant at the firm. She never ceased to motivate me. She is a wonderful wife and mother and friend. I knew in order to market and share my story, I needed to get on social media. She helped and encouraged me. She suggested I choose Facebook and she helped me. I have met so many wonderful people and made so many friends. When I lost my job after twenty-plus years, I also lost a little bit of trust in human nature. It brought me down to a new low. I do know that when one door closes another one opens and sometimes something bad like getting fired after a long time can look dreary at that moment, but a new, even better job came about, and new bright changes. I've gone along with those changes and I am hanging in there. Life goes on and I am going to get the best of it. I try to not look at what happened yesterday but instead what's happening today and plan a better tomorrow. It's hard to sometimes do this because I tend to dwell on things. But it's important to try our best to do it. I know because it truly helps keep a positive outlook and attitude. We all have pasts. We all have done things we are not proud of. We all made choices that weren't the best ones. But every day is a new day and we learn from our past and move forward to be a better person each and every day. And every day is a fresh start. That's all we can do.

BIO

My name is David Williams and I am the author of this story. Writing this book was a tough call, but I got it done. The Covid-19 Pandemic has taught me a few lessons. People need to step back and take a close look at what they have and not what they want. People need to take that extra step to really get to know their friends and people they thought were their friends. After getting fired, I had too much time on my hands. Like everyone else, I started to drink more cocktails than I should have. I stopped doing that and got a great new job and got really busy. I am doing excellent. My head is clear and my body feels good. But the lesson for this and a lot of goals is "One Day At A Time".

Believe me, it works. Many thanks for reading my book. Stay safe and God Bless You.

Much love,
David Williams